THE STOCK MARKET

By Donna Jo Fuller

Lerner Publications Company
Minneapolis

To my patient family and friends, with gratitude and hope

Special thanks to Marcia Marshall, Peg Goldstein, and my colleagues at Goldman Sachs for their generosity in sharing their knowledge and understanding.

The *Stock Market* has been written solely to offer information to children about the history of the stock market and about the basics of investing in the stock market. This book does not make any claims or guarantees that its information will help a child actually earn money through stock market investing. The author and publisher take no responsibility or liability in the success or failure of investment opportunities suggested by this book. When investing money, children and their parents should do the appropriate research into the market, funds, and financial services and consult qualified experts for advice on tax, legal, security, and other matters.

Lerner Publications Company
A division of Lerner Publishing Group
241 First Avenue North
Minneapolis, MN 55401 U.S.A.

Website address: www.lernerbooks.com

Library of Congress Cataloging-in-Publication Data

Fuller, Donna Jo
    The stock market / by Donna Jo Fuller
        p.   cm. — (How economics works)
    Includes bibliographical references and index.
    ISBN-13: 978-0-8225-2635-3 (lib. bdg. : alk. paper)
    ISBN-10: 0-8225-2635-2 (lib. bdg. : alk. paper)
    1. Stocks—Juvenile literature. 2. Stock exchanges—Juvenile literature.
    I. Title. II. Series.
    HG4661.F85 2006
    332.64'2—dc22   2005009798

Manufactured in the United States of America
1 2 3 4 5 6 – DP – 11 10 09 08 07 06

Table of Contents

CHAPTER 1
WHAT IS THE STOCK MARKET?

When Damon was six years old, he joined his parents' investment club. In this club, grown-ups and kids together studied a financial network called the stock market and researched companies. When Damon decided what companies he liked, his parents helped him buy stock, or part ownership, in those companies.

By the time Damon was nine, he owned stocks from twenty-five companies. Because the companies were successful, Damon had made thousands of dollars from his stocks. Damon figures he can pay half his college costs with the earnings from his investments.

Kids all over the country are studying the stock market and learning to earn money by investing, or buying stocks. You can, too.

THE COMPANY YOU KEEP

A company is a group of people working together to create something and sell it. A company may make and sell products, such as shoes and clothing. Or a company may sell a service, which means doing a job that people need done. For instance, some companies provide a service by delivering packages overnight.

This funny photograph from 1916 is an advertisement for Uneeda Biscuit ("You need a biscuit"), a product of the National Biscuit Company. In 1971 this company changed its name to Nabisco. In modern times, Nabisco's parent company, Kraft Foods Inc., sells its stock on the stock market.

Companies that want to grow bigger sometimes sell stock (also called shares of stock) on the stock market. By selling stock, the companies get extra money, which they can use to improve their businesses. In exchange for the money they pay for stock, the people who buy stock become part owners of the business. They also get to elect members of the company's board of directors—people who set the rules for running the business. People who own shares of stock are called stockholders or shareholders. People buy and sell shares of companies at stock exchanges.

The stock market is a network of stock exchanges, companies that sell stock, and shareholders who buy stock. The

Out with the Old

Before the days of computers, every person who bought stock received a stock certificate showing the name of the company, how many shares were bought on what date, and the name of the buyer. Stock certificates (below left) were made of thick paper with fancy lettering and special seals, or symbols pressed into the paper. These papers proved stock ownership, so they were very valuable. When a stockholder sold stock, he or she had to return the certificate. In modern times, companies no longer send stock certificates to shareholders, although you can still get one if you ask.

stock market isn't one big store or even a mall. It's located in different buildings and cities all around the world and on the Internet. The stock market is global.

Ups and Downs

Buying stock is an investment. When you invest, you spend money now with the hope of earning more money later. If you invest in a company and the company earns a profit (makes money), you can make money too. The company might give you a share of its profits, called a dividend. Or you might make money later by selling your stock for more than you paid for it in the first place. The extra money you make in the stock market is called your return.

Not all companies make money, however. Often companies do poorly, and the value of their stock falls, or goes down. When investors sell this stock, they receive less money than they paid for it. They could even lose all the money they invested. That is why the stock market is risky.

U.S. Stock Exchanges

In the United States, three main stock exchanges sell stock and other kinds of investments. The oldest and most famous is the New York Stock Exchange (NYSE), located in New York City. More than twenty-nine hundred companies trade stocks there. The American Stock Exchange (AMEX) is also based in New York City. Approximately eight hundred

MONEY TALK What do you do when you exchange? You trade one thing for another.

BANK ON IT The American Stock Exchange used to be called the New York Curb Market, because its members first traded outside on the curb. The exchange moved indoors in 1921. It was renamed the American Stock Exchange in 1953.

companies trade stocks on the AMEX. The Nasdaq Stock Market is another big stock exchange, with thirty-four hundred companies trading there. It is based in Rockville, Maryland.

At the NYSE and AMEX, people called traders work inside huge halls, called trading floors. There, traders sell different stocks at different trading stations. The Nasdaq, however, does not have a trading floor. Instead of working on a trading floor, Nasdaq traders buy and sell stock through a network of computers.

At stock exchanges, traders can see stock prices on big digital signs. The prices look like long strings of letters, numbers, and arrows. You've probably seen those

LEARN MORE ABOUT STOCK EXCHANGES

To learn more about stock exchanges, you can visit their websites. Here are web addresses for the three biggest U.S. stock exchanges:

American Stock Exchange: http://www.amex.com
Nasdaq Exchange: http://www.nasdaq.com
New York Stock Exchange: http://www.nyse.com

same symbols trailing across the bottom of your TV screen during news broadcasts. Another name for this trail is the ticker tape. The groups of letters (ticker symbols) on the ticker tape stand for company names. The numbers show current stock prices. The arrows are easy— they tell people whether the price of a stock has gone up or down since the day before.

A Little History

The U.S. stock market began in New York City in the late 1700s, when the United States was a new country. New York City was a thriving port and the main marketplace in the new nation. Ships docked there and unloaded goods from other nations.

Starting in 1790, a group of twenty-four men in New York City met regularly to buy and sell stocks. They held their meetings outside under a buttonwood tree. In 1792 they set rules about their buying and selling. They called their rules the Buttonwood Agreement, named for the tree where they met. That agreement was the beginning of the modern-day New York Stock Exchange.

Value Added

Before TV and computers, the ticker tape was a long, thin strip of paper. It came out of a machine (*below*) covered by a big glass dome. The machine was connected to a telegraph system, which sent stock prices and other information over electrical wires. The machine made ticking noises as it operated. The ticking sound and the strip of paper, or tape, gave the system its name.

This drawing of the New York Stock Exchange building *(center left)* in New York City was published in 1850.

In the 1800s, Americans built railroads, schools, factories, and cities from coast-to-coast. Many of the companies that built bridges, trains, ships, and buildings sold shares on the stock market. Banks, oil companies, and steel companies also sold shares on the stock market. The United States grew strong and wealthy. People made new inventions and created new ways of buying and selling. Many people bought items on credit, or borrowed money.

By the 1920s, the U.S. stock market was booming. Lots of people invested in the stock market because it seemed like a great way to make money. Some people and companies bought stock on credit, called buying on margin. When a lot of people want something, its price usually goes up. As more people invested, stock prices went higher and higher.

Then, in October 1929, people began to worry. They realized they were paying too much for stocks. All at once, thousands of people tried to sell their stocks. With so many sellers and not enough buyers, stock prices fell. On Tuesday, October 29, 1929, stock prices came crashing all the way down.

Suddenly, stock that had been worth thousands of dollars was worth nothing. People who had bought stock on margin couldn't pay their debts. Many investors lost all their money. Whole companies closed.

October 29, 1929, became known as Black Tuesday. It marked the beginning of the Great Depression, a worldwide economic downturn. During the Depression, businesses and banks closed. Thousands of people lost their jobs. Many people were hungry and homeless.

It took the United States more than ten years to recover from the Great Depression. After World War II (1939–1945), the stock market grew strong again. Although the stock market had some ups and downs, it remained strong throughout the rest of the 1900s.

During the Great Depression, places called soup kitchens served free food to jobless and homeless people.

CHAPTER 2
WHY TO BUY AND WHAT TO BUY

Why do people invest in the stock market? The answer is easy: to make money. Some people invest to make money for retirement. Retirement? You haven't even started a job yet—so you won't be retiring anytime soon. But you probably want money for other things. What are your goals?

ARE WE THERE YET?

Most people have short-term goals and long-term goals. In the short term, you might want to buy a new DVD. It won't take you very long to get the money to buy it. You can probably cover the cost with your allowance and the money you earn doing chores.

But suppose you want to buy a car when you're sixteen. Better yet, suppose you want to drive that car to college when you're eighteen. You're going to need a lot of money for those long-term goals. You can get that money, with the help of a parent, by investing in the stock market.

A young man drives a car in 1917. Many young people save money with the long-term goal of buying their first car.

WHO SELLS STOCK?

Not all companies sell stock on the stock market. Companies that are privately owned don't sell stock and don't share profits with investors. Some privately owned companies are very small, and some are large. They may be owned by a small group of coworkers or business partners, by a family, or by just one person. Their business dealings are kept private.

Companies that do sell shares on the stock market are called public companies. When a company decides to "go public," or sell stock, its business dealings become public knowledge. The company must file financial reports with the Securities and Exchange Commission, and these reports are available on the Internet and in other public places.

DreamWorks executives rang the opening bell at the New York Stock Exchange on October 28, 2004. That was the day DreamWorks Animation SKG "went public." That means investors can buy its stock. The bell-ringing ceremony starts the business day at 9:30 A.M. and closes the stock market at 4:00 P.M.

How Does Money Grow in the Stock Market?

You can make money in the stock market in different ways. First, you can make money by selling stocks for more than you paid for them. Suppose you invest in a company when it's small. Its stock costs only $5 per share, or unit. Over the years, the company grows big and prosperous. Everyone wants to own a piece of this successful business. Because the stock is so popular, the price goes up and up. Your stock that was once worth five dollars per share is worth fifty dollars per share. If you sell one share, you've made a profit of forty-five dollars. If you sell one hundred shares, your profit is fort-five hundred dollars!

DOLLARS & SENSE A U.S. government agency called the Securities and Exchange Commission (SEC) makes rules for the stock market. The SEC makes sure that companies and stock traders do business fairly and do not cheat or mislead investors.

Investors can make money other ways. Sometimes, when a company makes a profit, it gives some of the profit to shareholders. These dividends can be small or large—from less than one hundred dollars a year to several thousand dollars a year. The amount a shareholder receives depends on how many shares he or she owns.

Not all companies offer dividends, however. Some companies instead reinvest their profits into the business. In this way, a company can make better products and sell more of them. As the company grows stronger, its stock grows in value. Although the stockholders don't get dividends, their stock becomes more and more valuable.

When they decide to sell the stock, they'll make money. Some companies give shareholders more stock instead of dividends. That's good for stockholders too because more stock means more money when it's time to sell.

OTHER KINDS OF INVESTMENTS

You can buy more than just stocks in the stock market. Another kind of investment is a bond. Buying a bond is like making a loan to a company or to the government.

Here's how it works. Bond buyers lend money to an organization (a government or a company) for a specific time period, usually five, seven, or ten years. At the end of that time, the organization pays back the amount of the original loan, plus interest. Interest is a fee that borrowers pay to lenders. Interest is set as a percentage of the amount of money borrowed.

Imagine buying a ten-year bond for one thousand dollars, with 5 percent interest (the interest rate on a bond is called the coupon). During the next ten years, you'll get interest payments of 5 percent of one thousand dollars (fifty dollars) each year. After ten years, you'll get your original one thousand dollars back, plus you'll have received fifty dollars each year for ten years. That extra five hundred dollars is your interest— a payment for lending money to the organization that sold you the bond.

The U.S., state, and city governments often sell bonds. They use money from the sale of bonds to pay for new roads, schools, or other projects. Companies

Bonds help to pay for the construction of new schools.

sell bonds too. Companies sell bonds when they need extra money but don't want to sell more shares of stock.

People who buy bonds are called bondholders. Unlike stockholders, they are not part owners of the company that sells them bonds. Bonds are bought and sold on stock exchanges, just like stock and other kinds of investments.

PUT YOUR EGGS IN DIFFERENT BASKETS

People often warn one another: don't put all your eggs in one basket! Why not? Because if you're walking along with your basket of eggs and you trip over a tree root, you'll break all those eggs. What do you have then? Nothing.

How can you prevent losing everything? When it comes to investing, the answer is to diversify, or spread out, your investments. Your portfolio—or group of investments—should consist of different kinds of stocks,

To invest wisely, many people buy different types of investments. Putting all your eggs in one basket—or buying only one type of stock—is risky.

bonds, and other investments. In that way, if one investment does poorly, you'll still have others that might do well. You won't be in danger of losing all your money on a bad investment.

A good way to diversify your portfolio is to invest in mutual funds. A mutual fund is a company that pools (gathers together) money from many different investors, then uses the money to buy lots of different stocks, bonds, and other kinds of investments. For the investor, investing in a mutual fund can be a smart choice. For one thing, a mutual fund has a big pool of money, so it can buy more stocks and bonds than you could buy on your own. And even if some stocks in the fund don't do well, others will probably grow in value. Finally, the people who run mutual funds are experts. They research, buy, and sell stocks and bonds full-time. They study the economy and the stock market and talk to each other about economic trends. You can usually count on them to make good decisions about investing your money.

CHAPTER 3
MARKET TRENDS

Have you ever heard a TV announcer say, "The Dow is down" or "the S&P is up"? What do those talking heads mean? "The Dow" refers to the Dow Jones Industrial Average. "S&P" is short for Standard and Poor's 500.

The Dow and the S&P are called stock indexes. The Nasdaq Stock Market has a stock index too. A stock index is a group of stocks. Financial journalist Charles Dow and his business partner Edward Jones invented the first stock index, the Dow Jones Industrial Average, in 1896. The Dow Jones Industrial Average includes only thirty stocks—from thirty of the biggest companies in the United States. The S&P has five hundred stocks (just like its name says). The Nasdaq has all the stocks trading on the Nasdaq Stock Market— more than thirty-four hundred.

Every day, stock analysts figure out the average of the prices or the values of the stocks in each stock index. They use computers and mathematical equations to convert the averages into points (for instance, the Dow Jones Industrial Average is more than 10,000 points). Then analysts report the points in the newspaper, on TV and radio, and on the Internet. They also compare

MONEY TALK When a newscaster says, "Volume was heavy today," does that person mean that people put on weight? If the newscaster says, "Volume was light," did those same people go on a diet? Well, maybe they did, but "volume was heavy" actually means that lots of people are buying and selling stocks and bonds. "Volume was light" means it was a slow day for stock trading.

A 1960s radio announcer makes a stock market report. Modern radio broadcasters still report on the stock market every day.

the daily average of each index to its average from the day before.

By looking at a group of stocks instead of just one, analysts can see how the stock market is behaving as a whole. If index averages go up, it means prices are rising, because lots of people are buying stocks. People think they can

A Nasdaq Composite Index report flashes on an outdoor electronic billboard in New York City. The sign shows the "point" level of the index and that it's down from the day before. The last number is the volume of Nasdaq trading for the day.

make money by investing. If the index averages go down, that means prices are dropping, because people are selling more than they're buying. They might be worried that investing is too risky, so they don't buy stocks.

THE BIG PICTURE

Stock prices go up and down for many reasons. Suppose two Japanese stereo makers talk about merging into one company. When investors hear about the possible merger, the stock prices of both companies may go down. Why? Because investors can't be sure how much longer each company will continue to do business on its own. Investing in the unknown is risky.

Suppose the U.S. government is investigating a drug company to make sure that its products are safe. How will the investigation turn out? What if the drugs are unsafe and the government punishes the company? Investors don't want to take a chance on a company that might be heading for trouble. So the company's stock price might fall.

But the stock market depends on more than just business news. Current events also influence the stock market. When investors feel confident about the government,

MONEY TALK Perhaps you've heard about a "bear market" or a "bull market." What are bears and bulls doing in the stock market? A "bear market" means stock prices are going down. A "bull market" means stock prices are going up.

Why bears and bulls? Bears kill their prey by swooping down with their claws. Bulls gore their victims by striking up with their horns!

the economy, jobs, and the future, they are likely to buy more stocks. When they are worried about these same things, they might sell stocks. When there's a war or economic trouble in the nation or the world, people don't want to take chances with their money.

On Tuesday, September 11, 2001, terrorists attacked targets in the United States. One of the attacks took place near the stock exchanges in New York City. Many financial businesses were destroyed or damaged. The stock exchanges closed for almost a week. Because investors were worried, they bought fewer stocks. Stock prices fell.

In March 2003, the United States went to war against Iraq, a nation in the Middle East. At first, people were confident that the United States would easily win the war. Stock prices went up. Within a few months, though, stock prices started dropping. People realized the war was not going to be over quickly. War makes people worry about the future.

Terrorists hijacked four passenger planes on September 11, 2001. They crashed two of the planes into the towers of the World Trade Center *(far right, smoking)* in New York City.

BUBBLES BURSTING IN AIR

Stock market crashes (remember 1929?) usually happen after a "bubble." In the stock market, a bubble is a time of rising prices. Bubbles look pretty, but when they get too big, they burst.

In the late 1990s, many people bought stock in dot-com companies—new companies that did business over the Internet. Many people thought the new Internet businesses would thrive. They thought they could make a lot of money by investing in this new kind of business. So

In this political cartoon from 1901, the bull blowing bubbles *(left)* represents the stock market. The bull is also a cartoon of John Pierpont Morgan, one of the biggest stockholders in many successful railroads and steel mills in the late 1800s. By 1901 stocks in these businesses were very expensive. Yet investors *(right)* strain to grab stock market bubbles—stock investments like Morgan's.

many people bought dot-com stocks that prices skyrocketed. But most dot-com companies did not succeed. By 2000 many of the companies had failed. The bubble burst. Dot-com stock prices dropped dramatically. Investors lost a lot of money.

LOOK INTO YOUR CRYSTAL BALL?

Some people devote their whole careers to watching stock market trends. They study stock indexes, current events, and business news to figure out what the stock market might do in the future. Some people become experts on a certain kind of stock or a certain business area, such as

BANK ON IT In the 1990s, an average of 290 million shares of stock changed hands (were bought and sold) each day. The stocks were all traded in U.S. stock exchanges, but the investors were people from around the world. By 2004 the average was 1.4 billion shares traded each day.

Brokers study overhead computer screens full of stock market information.

These alphabet cubes spell out investors' choices. Investors must do their homework to decide whether to buy, sell, or hold (keep) a stock.

food, computers, or athletic shoes.

But even the most experienced stock analysts don't have all the answers. After all, unless you happen to own a crystal ball, it's impossible to know for sure whether a certain stock price will go up or down. It's also hard to predict wars and other current events that might affect the stock market. That's why investing in the stock market will always be risky.

CHAPTER 4
HOW TO INVEST

People, businesses, governments, and other organizations can all invest in the stock market. With the help of a parent, you can invest too! But where should you invest your money?

Maybe you want to invest in a big, famous athletic shoe company because you like to wear its shoes. Since the company is successful, you might think investing in it will be a sure thing. But lots of other people probably want to invest in such a famous and successful company too. So its stock price will probably be high. If you buy high-priced stock and the company hits hard times, you could lose a lot of money.

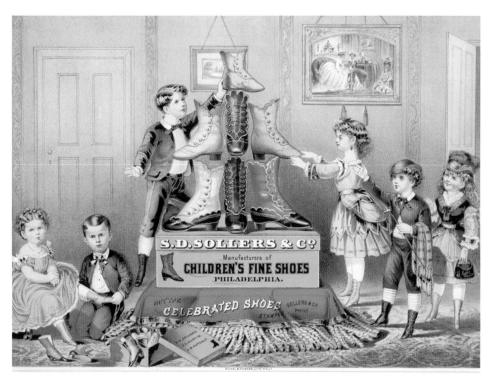

This advertisement from 1874 promotes a shoe company that is no longer in business. But some companies from the 1870s are still going strong. How can investors predict how a company might perform in the long run?

What about investing in a small, unknown company? Since the company is not famous or popular, you might be able to buy its stock for a low price. And that little company could grow from a tiny seed into a really big apple. If so, the price of your stock will go up, and you will make a lot of money. But what if the company doesn't grow? In five years, you might end up with a lot of stock that isn't worth anything.

It's easy to see that investing is risky business. You might win big. But you can lose big too. How do you lessen the risk? You can start by picking good investments.

DO YOUR HOMEWORK

Before you buy a stock, it's important to research the company. What does the company sell? Who buys its products? Does the company have a good reputation? How long has it been in business? What other companies sell the same thing? Of all the companies that sell the same thing, which company does a better job? Investigate!

Remember, your research should include learning about current events. What's happening in the company's industry—its overall business area, such as fast food, clothing, or electronics. Perhaps you've read in the

Handheld music players are among the most successful products in the consumer electronics category. Companies that make the devices have seen their stock value rise.

newspapers that people are suing a fast-food chain for serving fattening food. This kind of bad publicity could make the stock price go down. Maybe you've read that natural foods are the trend of the future. So you might want to invest in a company that sells natural foods instead of one that sells fast foods.

You can learn a lot about a company on its website. There you can find the company's ticker symbol and find out which stock exchange trades its stocks. You can also find the company's annual report, a yearly summary of its business activities. The annual report will include five years of the company's financial history. Ask an adult to help you figure out the numbers in the report. Has the company's net worth (how much money it has after expenses are paid) grown over the years? Ten percent growth a year is great! Have the company's expenses gone up over the last five years? Down is better!

GUESS THE TICKER SYMBOLS

Here's a list of ticker symbols for some of the most famous companies in the world. Can you guess what company each symbol stands for? The answers are on page 42. Don't peek!

1. AAPL
2. ATVI
3. DWA

4. GOOG
5. MCD
6. NKE

Tracking Your Stock

Open the newspaper to the business section and find the listing for your favorite stock. Run your finger along the row (or use a ruler) and find the column labeled "Last." The number you'll find there is yesterday's price for the stock, also called a quote. Write down quotes for the stock for ten business days. That's two weeks. Stock exchanges close for the weekend, so stock prices don't change then.

Next, plot the price changes on a piece of graph paper. On the left side of the paper, draw a vertical (up-and-down) line. Mark different prices evenly along the line—the lowest on the bottom, the highest on top. At the bottom of the vertical line, draw a horizontal line, left to right. Write dates along this line, evenly spaced from left to right. Next, make dots on your graph, corresponding to the stock's price each day, and connect the dots. Your graph will look something like this:

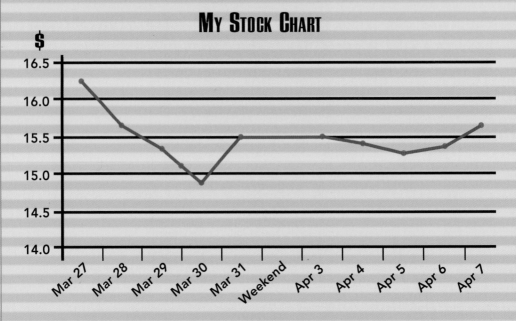

My Stock Chart

There! You've created a stock chart. Is the price going up or down?

You can get even more financial information on websites such as www.marketwatch.com, www.money.cnn.com, and www.investorguide.com. Each site is organized a little differently. To research a company, look for a box that says "quote" or "research" and type in the company's ticker symbol. If you don't know the ticker symbol, you can look that up on the website too. Typing in the ticker symbol will lead you to lots of information about the company. You'll learn about the company's financial history, how many people work there, and how many shares of its stock are traded in the stock market. The website will allow you to compare the company with its competitors. You'll also find links to news stories about the company and other financial documents.

Value Added

Many websites offer information on stocks and investing. Here is a list of some of the most well-known sites:

CNN Money:
http://www.money.cnn.com
Investopedia:
http://www.investopedia.com
Investor Guide:
http://www.investorguide.com
Market Watch:
http://www.marketwatch.com
MSN Money:
http://www.moneycentral.msn.com
The Motley Fool:
http://www.fool.com
Smart Money:
http://www.smartmoney.com

The daily newspaper will give you even more information. Turn to the business section. You'll see a list of stocks—so many that the newspaper has to use tiny print to fit them all. Find the ticker symbol for your company and look across the row at the listing. (A ruler might come in handy here.) You'll see columns labeled "52-Week High" and "52-Week Low." The year has fifty-two weeks, and these numbers show you the highest and

WALL STREET AND THE *WALL STREET JOURNAL*

New York City started as a small settlement on the southern tip of Manhattan Island. In 1653 the townspeople built a wall to protect themselves from Native American and European enemies. The wall was later replaced by a road, called Wall Street. The street was short, running only a few blocks. But it later became home to big stock exchanges—the New York Stock Exchange and the American Stock Exchange—as well as to important banks.

In 1889 Dow Jones and Company, founded by business owners Charles Dow and Edward Jones, first published a newspaper devoted to financial news. All the important U.S. banks and stock exchanges were located on Wall Street, so Dow and Jones called the newspaper the *Wall Street Journal*. The two men also created the Dow Jones Industrial Average and other stock indexes.

The *Wall Street Journal* first published only stock prices and financial news. It then added articles about politics, culture, science, and other subjects. In modern times, the paper has one of the highest circulations (number of readers) of any U.S. newspaper. It is still published by Dow Jones and Company.

lowest prices of the stock over the past year. Compare those numbers to the stock's current price—listed in a column labeled "Last"—the price of the stock when the market closed at 4 P.M. the day before. If the stock pays a dividend, you can find the yearly amount per share in a column labeled "Div." An important number is found in a column labeled "P/E." This number compares the stock price to the real worth of the company.

Understanding all the numbers won't be easy. Some people study for many years to learn about the stock market and how to analyze investments. Many people hire experts to pick stocks for them. You don't have to be an expert to invest in the stock market, but the more information you gather, the better your chances of succeeding.

MONEY TALK There are many ways to analyze stocks. The price-to-earnings (P/E) ratio is one good measuring tool. A ratio is a comparison between two numbers. A P/E ratio compares the price of a stock to the earnings of the company. Newspapers publish P/E ratios every day. Look in the business section for your favorite stock's P/E ratio. If the ratio is high, say 40 to 50, then the stock might be overpriced. If the number is low, between 18 and 25, then the price is right.

KIDS AND INVESTING

Once you've analyzed companies and think you've found a winner, you're ready to invest. You can't buy stocks on your own (you must be eighteen to do that), but you can invest with the help of your parents or grandparents.

They can create an account for you at a brokerage house, or broker, a company that buys and sells stocks. The people who work at the brokerage house will do the actual trades, but you can decide what to buy or sell.

There are several kinds of brokerage houses. Full-service brokers help their clients set goals and choose investments. They help people decide how to invest and what stocks and bonds to buy and sell. They advise clients about changes in the stock market and how to improve their portfolios. Full-service brokers do all the buying and selling for their clients.

An investor *(left)* discusses his portfolio with his broker.

Your Stock File

When you research a company, mark down the information you find on a chart like this:

My Stock File

Company's name: _____

Ticker symbol:_____

Exchange the company trades on: _____

What the company makes or does: _____

The company's industry: _____

Do I use the company's products or services? _____

Does my family use the company's products or services? _____

P/E ratio: _____

Competitor's P/E ratio: _____

Company's net worth five years ago: _____

Company's net worth this year: _____

Notes about whether or not this stock might be a good investment:

_____

_____

_____

_____

_____

_____

Discount brokers also buy and sell for clients, but they do less advising. Clients of discount brokers must do their own research and decide how to meet their own financial goals. Full-service brokers charge more than discount brokers, because they do more work for clients.

Online brokerage houses allow people to buy and sell their own stocks on the Internet. These companies usually charge less than other brokers because clients get even less help and advice.

Some brokerage houses have special programs for kids. For example, some brokers allow kids to invest in mutual funds with very little money. Some brokers allow kids to set up automatic investment plans, which involve investing just a little money each month. You'll need a parent's help to participate in any of these programs.

It is convenient to buy and sell stock from a computer at home. Remember, a parent must supervise a young person using the Internet in this way.

When you make an investment in a company, computers at the brokerage house will record your purchase and keep track of your stock. The brokerage house will send you statements, or reports, four times a year. These reports will tell you the company's value at the end of each quarter (one-fourth of a year) and the value of each share of your stock. Twice a year, you'll receive more detailed reports about the company's finances.

MAKING THE TEAM

You and your friends—perhaps your soccer or softball team—might want to form an investment club. Club members can research companies as a group and gather more information than you likely could do on your own. You can share and compare information, choose investments, pool your money, and then—with the help of an adult—invest in the stock market.

TIMELINE

1792 New York traders sign the Buttonwood Agreement, creating the New York Stock Exchange. The first company whose stock is traded on the exchange is the Bank of New York.

1830 The first railroad stock is traded on the New York Stock Exchange.

CA. 1849 The New York Curb Market opens in New York. Its members meet outside on the curb.

1867 The first ticker tape machine is created.

1878 The first telephone is installed on the New York Stock Exchange trading floor.

1889 The Dow Jones Company begins publishing the *Wall Street Journal.*

1896 Charles Dow invents the first stock index, the Dow Jones Industrial Average. The index begins with twelve stocks and a value of 40 points.

1906 The Dow Jones Industrial Average tops 100 points for the first time.

1921 The New York Curb Market moves from the curb to indoor offices.

1923 A "bull market"—a time of rising stock prices—begins in the United States.

1929 The stock market crashes on October 29, called Black Tuesday. The Great Depression begins.

1934 The Securities and Exchange Commission is formed. The commission's job is to prohibit stock market fraud and to make sure companies reveal complete information about stocks and bonds to investors.

1953 The New York Curb Market changes its name to the American Stock Exchange.

1971 The Nasdaq Stock Market, the world's first electronic stock exchange, is established.

1999 The Dow Jones Industrial Average tops 10,000 points for the first time.

2000 On January 14, the Dow closes at its all-time high: 11,722 points. Later in the year, the dot-com bubble bursts, causing many investors to lose money.

2001 Terrorists strike targets in New York City and Washington, D.C., on September 11. The stock market closes. When it reopens on September 17, it sets a new record: 2.37 billion shares traded in one day.

2005 An average of 1.7 billion shares of stock are traded in the stock market each day.

GLOSSARY

annual report: a yearly summary of a company's finances and business activities

bond: an investment that involves making a loan to a government or business. People buy bonds to earn interest.

broker: a person or company that buys and sells stocks for clients

bubble: a time of rising stock prices, often ending with a collapse

company: a group of people who work together to create and sell a product or service

credit: borrowed money

debt: money that is owed to someone else

dividend: a share of a company's profits

interest: the price someone pays for the temporary use of someone else's money

invest: to set aside or spend money in the hope of earning more money in the future

loss: a decrease in wealth, sometimes as a result of selling stock for a lower price than one paid for it originally

margin: borrowed money, or credit

mutual fund: a company that uses money from many different investors to buy stocks, bonds, and other kinds of investments

ANSWERS FOR GAME ON PAGE 31

1. Apple Computer Inc.
2. Activision, Inc.
3. DreamWorks Animation
4. Google Inc.
5. McDonald's Corporation
6. Nike Inc.

portfolio: an individual's group of stocks, bonds, and other investments

profit: an increase in wealth, sometimes as a result of selling stock for a higher price than one paid for it originally

public companies: companies that sell shares on the stock market

quote: the price of a stock at the end of the previous business day

return: profit made from an investment, such as the sale of stock

share: a unit of stock

stock: a share, or part ownership, of a company

stock analyst: a broker, bank employee, or investment adviser who studies companies, sometimes specializing in a sector or industry. Analysts use many techniques to research and make buy/sell recommendations. Traders and investors may use an analyst's published research to help them make decisions.

stock exchange: an organization that trades stocks. The three big U.S. stock exchanges are the New York Stock Exchange, the American Stock Exchange, and the Nasdaq Stock Market.

stock index: a group of stocks, whose prices are averaged to determine overall market trends

stock market: the worldwide network of stock exchanges, stock brokers, investors, and companies that sell stocks

ticker tape: a running display of stock symbols and prices that appears inside stock exchanges and on some TV news shows

trader: a person who works at a stock exchange, buying and selling stocks

volume: the number of stocks or bonds bought and sold within a specific period of time. Trading volume can refer to the volume of trading of a single company's stock or for an entire stock exchange.

BIBLIOGRAPHY

Little, Jeffrey B., and Lucien Rhodes. *Understanding Wall Street.* 3rd ed. New York: Liberty Hall Press, 1991.

Lynch, Peter, and John Rothchild. *Learn to Earn: A Beginner's Guide to the Basics of Investing and Business.* New York: Simon & Schuster, 1995.

Mladjenovic, Paul. *Stock Investing for Dummies.* New York: Hungry Minds, Inc., 2002.

Morris, Kenneth M., and Virginia B. Morris. *Your Guide to Understanding Investing.* New York: Lightbulb Press, Inc., 1999.

Slavin, Steve. *Economics: A Self-Teaching Guide.* 2nd ed. New York: John Wiley & Sons, Inc., 1999.

Smith, Pat, and Lynn Roney. *Wow the Dow! The Complete Guide to Teaching Your Kids How to Invest in the Stock Market.* New York: Simon & Schuster, 2000.

FURTHER READING

Bamford, Janet. *StreetWise: A Guide for Teen Investors.* Princeton, NJ: Bloomberg Press, 2000.

Berg, Adriane C., and Arthur Berg Bochner. *The Totally Awesome Business Book for Kids.* New York: Newmarket Press, 1995.

Blumenthal, Karen. *Six Days in October: The Stock Market Crash of 1929.* New York: Atheneum Books for Young Readers, 2002.

Godfrey, Neale S. *Neale S. Godfrey's Ultimate Kids' Money Book.* New York: Simon & Schuster Books for Young Readers, 1998.

Mayr, Diane. *The Everything Kids' Money Book.* Avon, MA: Adams Media Corp., 2000.

McGowan, Eileen Nixon, and Nancy Lagow Dumas. *Stock Market Smart.* Brookfield, CT: Millbrook Press, 2002.

Otfinoski, Steve. *The Kid's Guide to Money.* New York: Scholastic, Inc., 1996.

WEBSITES

Kid's Savings Calculator
　　http://www.investoreducation.org
　　Click on "Kid's Savings Calculator" under "Young Investors."

Created by the Alliance for Investor Education, this site shows how your money can grow if you save it in the bank instead of spending it right away.

Kidstock
http://www.kidstock.com
Kids and their parents can learn about stocks, bonds, banks, and money in general, and plan for a college education at this site.

Stock Market Game
http://www.smg2000.org
The Stock Market Game gives players a hands-on chance to learn about investing by making up a one-hundred-thousand-dollar real-time portfolio.

StocksQuest: A Global Stock Market Game
http://www.stocksquest.com
The site includes a virtual stock market game, which lets players practice their investing skills without spending any real money.

YoungBiz Better Investing Workshops
http://www.youngbiz.com
Teaming with the National Association of Investors Corporation, YoungBiz offers online workshops covering stocks, research, indexes, and saving.

Young Investors
http://www.younginvestor.com/kids
This site provides lots of basics on investing, indexes, research, and mutual funds. It includes games and puzzles and even teaches visitors how to talk about the stock market in Spanish!

Sights to Visit

Fed Center, San Francisco, California
http://www.frbsf.org/federalreserve/people/index.html#sf
The Federal Reserve is a government agency that oversees the U.S. banking system. Fed Center, located at the San Francisco branch of the Federal Reserve, is a hands-on museum with exhibits about money and banking.

Museum of American Financial History, New York, New York
http://www.financialhistory.org
The Museum of American Financial History, located in New York City in the Wall Street area, is associated with the Smithsonian Institution. Founded in 1988, the financial museum offers exhibits on the history of banking, business, and businesspeople in the United States.

INDEX

ABOUT THE AUTHOR

Donna Jo (DJ) Fuller has worked for more than a decade in a Wall Street investment banking firm, specializing in mutual funds. DJ is a native New Yorker—born, bred, and schooled there. Before working on Wall Street, DJ worked in publishing and the theater, where she toured the United States and Germany as an actor. She juggles her work on Wall Street with acting in and directing plays in New York City.

PHOTO ACKNOWLEDGMENTS

The images in this book are used with the permission of: Library of Congress, pp. 5 (LC-USZ62-98473), 10 (LC-USZ62-116336), 13 (LC-DIG-nclc-04036), 25 (LC-USZC4-7880), 29 (LC-USZC4-2057); PhotoDisc Royalty Free by Getty Images, pp. 6, 34; © Independent Picture Service, p. 9; © National Archives, p. 11; © PETER MORGAN/Reuters/CORBIS, p. 14; © Robert W. Kelley/Time Life Pictures/Getty Pictures, p. 17; © Sucre Sale/SuperStock, p. 18; © age fotostock/SuperStock, pp. 21, 26, 27, 38; Minnesota Historical Society, p. 22; © Reuters NewMedia Inc./CORBIS, p. 24; © Todd Strand/Independent Picture Service, p. 30; © Ed Bock/CORBIS, p. 36.

The illustrations on pp. 1, 4, 12, 20, 28, front cover and back cover are by Bill Hauser. Back cover: Hypnoclips (both)